Publisher: Travis Rigby

Author: Julia Rose

Editor: Jon Bell

Graphic Designer: Kathleen Dillinger

2023, WildFlower Media, Inc.

Printed in India

ISBN 978-1-7355603-7-3

COLOUR MY WORLD

by *Julia Rose*

JOY, CREATIVITY
AND A LIFE SURROUNDED
BY FLOWERS

CONTENTS

p. 6

PREFACE

p. 9

INTRODUCTION

p. 10

PLANTING THE SEEDS

p. 16

A JOURNEY OF EXPLORATION

p. 24

NEW CREATIONS

p. 32

BACK OUT IN THE WORLD

p. 36

FLORAL FASHION ON
A GRAND SCALE

p. 57

ON THE FARM

p. 68

REMEMBERING POSSUM
AND FINDING HAPPINESS

p. 72

VIGNETTES OF CREATIVITY

p. 82

MAKING THE MAGIC

p. 108

INDEX

p. 110

ACKNOWLEDGEMENTS

p. 112

ABOUT THE AUTHOR

PREFACE

Flowers are my medium. They are my paint or clay, my tulle, chiffon and sequins.

I envision my pieces in my mind, then they pour through my fingers until they come to life. The pieces are momentary, making the capture key. This allows me to introduce multiple layers of art to the vision.

A mood, an emotion, a concept is first. What is it I want to say?

Next comes the colour palette, relaying emotion through colour. A great colour palette speaks a thousand words.

Then the floral recipe. I love depth and heavy texture. Lashing the greenery into the design like heavy paint or massed tulle. Greenery creates my base movement. After that, the flowers. Imagine tiny sweet blooms nestled atop big, fat, mass petalled flowers; blocking flowers for colour pops; and feathering flowers for those delicate features.

Now for the canvas: the model. From the colour of the skin to the line of the jaw, the length of the arms and the curve of the body, it all comes into play when dramatizing and pushing the desired mood.

The final step is the capture. Painting the whole piece with the right light. Setting the mood and connecting the piece to the viewer, relaying emotion, making someone feel through the piece, hearing it speak.

When I can make someone feel with my art, I have succeeded. Creating is something I have to do to feel whole. Every creation has a piece of me in it.

"Learn the rules
like a pro, so you
can break them
like an artist."

Pablo Picasso

"Imagination is more
important than knowledge.
Knowledge is limited.
Imagination encircles
the world."

Albert Einstein

INTRODUCTION

This is the story of how my art is born.

I come from humble beginnings, a large hard-working family.
My grandfather was a soldier, and my grandmother raised many
children. She fed us well and loved Elvis, her garden and the arts.
She taught us that small things make for a happy heart.

Like the miracle of a single flower.

As you will learn in this book, my skills have developed and
evolved throughout the years. A combination of life experiences
has presented me with my own unique style, my craft and artistic
talent. This book touches on the artistic life that has led my creative
self to this point.

As the saying goes, "Every flower must grow through dirt."

I know it is my darkness that has made me shine – my ability to look
at the bright side of every situation, learn lessons, grow, and always
embrace all that is oneself.

I have found beauty in every aspect of my life.

I do not fit into one niche. I have been likened to a circus performer.
That may have been meant as an insult, but perspective, right?

I'm imagining some glorious rock-show-style circus with fireworks,
heavy red curtains, a smoke machine, and all the wild, fantastical
theatrics that make one's heart flutter.

It brings me such joy to share this circus with the world. I revel in the
thought of evoking a sense of freedom for all to be the amazing
beings that you can be.

Come join me for the ride. I hope you enjoy viewing my creations as
much as I enjoyed creating them. Let's dive in and rock this!

PLANTING

THE

SEEDS

My grandmother loved flowers. She was creative, she was crafty. I remember we'd go to the local church in Newcastle, a harbour city in eastern Australia, and have our flowers read – similar to how you have your tea leaves read. We'd choose a flower from the garden and take it along with us, and a lady would tell us wonderful things, all according to the flower. Looking back, I really think it was an excuse to drink tea and eat cake whilst surrounded by flowers.

Nan and Pop loved gardening. My job was to relocate the snails out of the garden. I always used to take the thorns of my grandfather's prize roses and stick them to my nose, pretending I was a rhinoceros. I loved hiding in the cavernous branches of my grandmother's *Hydrangea*, looking up at the dappled sunlight and the big beautiful blooms, watching little spiders make webs that would catch the light and shine like rainbows.

This was the 1970s, and back then, the streets of Newcastle were lined with fruit trees and the gardens were abundant in flowers, old-fashioned flowers like snapdragons and stock roses – all of that beautiful English garden style.

I remember walking the streets with my auntie and mother. We'd eat fruit from the trees and pick flowers from the gardens to put in our hair. A big fat garden rose, abundant in petals and sweet in perfume, would be perfect. Daisies or clovers would make for a sweet little flower crown to wear for the day. And jasmine was a favourite. A couple of those sweet little flowers in our hair, and the scent would follow us around all day. There's nothing like the sweet perfume of a jasmine bloom in a hot summer breeze.

When I was 16, I was in a car accident. I went through a windscreen. I had 48 stitches in my face. You can only imagine how that felt as a teenager. I went back and lived with my nana. My auntie got me a job as a trainee florist in Newcastle. It was the perfect place to be, surrounded by beauty. I worked hard scrubbing buckets and learning all the basics, serving customers, bringing the flowers out and putting them away.

From there I went on to be a junior and do a traineeship in floristry. At the age of 21, I had all my qualifications and was a certified florist, so I packed up and headed off on an adventure of travel for the next five years.

A JOURNEY
OF
EXPLORATION

I explored the east coast of Australia, working in all different fields. One of my jobs was working as a party motivator. What is a party motivator you may ask? Well, it's someone who encourages people to have fun. I loved it. It was the perfect job for me because I love making people happy. I love seeing people happy. That job also let me be creative and express myself.

One venue I worked at was set in the middle of the Daintree Rainforest, a UNESCO World Heritage Site far from civilization. In those years, one would have to cross the crocodile-filled Daintree River by ferry, then travel an hour or two along a narrow, winding road that turned into a dirt track until finally reaching the Jungle Village. It was a big, beautiful venue; imagine Tarzan's hut, but bigger! It was similar to an oversized log cabin with no walls – just hot, tropical, balmy jungle weather walls. It wasn't too fancy, just fabulous, raw and rustic, with a jungle atmosphere in every aspect.

The main venue was surrounded by 20 to 30 smaller log cabins where guests, mostly backpackers, would stay. Every Tuesday, a bus full of more than 200 backpackers arrived for party night – a night of party games and festivities. We would hand out paper bags, body paint and palm fronds. Everyone was encouraged to come in fancy dress. I worked in the main bar area, where I would help people with their costume designs, serve drinks and, generally, be a little wild and extroverted, encouraging people to dance, laugh, dress up and have fun.

During the off-season, I worked as a snorkel tour guide on the Great Barrier Reef. During one off-season, I lived on a World Heritage Site island and worked at a five-star resort off the coast of tropical northern Queensland. On my days off, I would wander the reef and rainforest of the island, gathering beauties from nature and making jewellery and art to sell when I'd get back to the mainland.

"Makeup was heavy,
with rouged cheeks
and lipstick to match."

Another job that I had during the off-season was at a theatre restaurant that an American couple owned. Every time I would head back to the Gold Coast, I worked here. We used to perform on-stage events in the city, in public areas. It was another job that inspired and brought smiles to strangers, but it wasn't all about the other people. It brought me so much joy as I got to express myself and be a weirdo in the most fabulous of ways. My role was a wench, which occasionally included performing as a backup belly dancer. Everyone who booked for the theatre restaurant would be given a medieval costume to wear. I would encourage people to have fun and help relax them by being a little cheeky. My costume consisted of a tightly bound corset with a lace-up bustier and a layered bustle skirt. It took some time in the dressing room to get in and out of this attire – and there was no quick escape at the end of the night! Makeup was heavy, with rouged cheeks and lipstick to match.

After everyone was in costume, we'd take them up into the castle for a feast, a live stage show, and an interactive performance experience. Guests would drink and feast whilst we would perform, enticing them to let loose and interact with us, taking on their characters, too. We'd sing and dance and drag people onto stage. Every night was a whirlwind of fun where I could dive into the world of my character and inspire others to be free, too. It was great to think you'd given someone an experience that he or she would remember for a long time.

In between, I would sell art paintings and sculptures at markets and a little store. I worked at florists on Valentine's Day, Mother's Day, Christmas – all of those big days – and I got my floral skills up to date whilst exploring and expanding my creativity in different avenues. I worked with backpackers, I worked at five-star resorts, I did it all. I worked in bars, made beds, picked fruit. I didn't care what it was as long as it made me a dollar and kept me on my creative journey.

During this time, I met so many inspirational people from all different backgrounds and cultures, of all different colours. It helped me see beauty in the world in another way. The only things I needed to be happy were nature and my creativity. Those two things alone made my soul sing. A walk through the rainforest, a stroll along the beach, painting a picture, weaving, carving and sculpting always made me happy. If I was ever unhappy, I would do one of those things to express myself. We all know a long walk really can change your mood and mindset. Being in nature is incredible and so important to me. In fact, I lived in the Daintree Rain-forest for three months a year, for three years. That really connected me with nature. Mother Nature is my inspiration because, really, who does it better?

Once my journey of exploration had come to an end, I decided that I was going to be an adult – I mean a real adult – and get a real full-time job and buy a house and have some children. I took a full-time job with a florist, where I became the wedding specialist. It was a big florist, with five shops, and I worked in the main shop creating bouquets and arrangements to fill all five of the shops alongside a team of amazing and inspirational women. I was doing well on the track to becoming a good adult. Five years working 9 to 5, the beautiful surrounds of retail floristry. I loved it.

But life had a different plan.

NEW CREATIONS

I became very ill with a rare condition called chemical hypersensitivity. Basically, it's when you become allergic to the modern world. I was allergic to everything: perfume, car exhaust, moisturizers, hairspray – everything that everyone used every day, including all kinds of chemicals in food. My nose and throat would swell from something as simple as the person in front of me at the supermarket having washed his or her hair. I couldn't go outside without a mask. (This was long before COVID-19.)

It got to the point that it became impossible to live a normal adult life anymore.

I ended up having to quit my job and move to a tiny new house. It was very hypoallergenic-styled: large white tiles, a big air conditioning system, and just really sterile. I lived there for two-and-a-half years and became like a real-life bubble girl.

But instead of being the sick person that I was supposed to be with this issue, I decided I was going to do what I do best: create. I was going to create, purely to bring myself joy.

I had a little conure parrot named Pepe, two cats, Minkie and Mr. Meowie, and a dog, Rosie, who kept me company. They were perfect. They adored me and entertained me, and I loved them in return.

At the same time, my perspective on life changed. All of a sudden, life had become so fragile, and being a real adult didn't really seem to matter. What good was having an abundance of money if I wasn't alive to enjoy it? And what good was living a life that, really, I was living only to please other people?

Creating and nature made me happy, so that's what I did. I created for the pure sake of creation. I created because it brought me joy. I didn't care what anyone else's opinion of me was. As long as I was happy, that was all that mattered.

I was creating floral couture, in a certain way. At the time, large decadent headpieces were not on trend at all. Actually, people would scoff at me for creating them. I did not care. They brought me joy, and that was all I needed.

I did not design to traditional floristry rules. Even though I knew all the rules, I implemented them in my own fashion. I combined my love of art and theatre into the pieces, intertwining costume, fashion, theatre, and arts. Flowers were my medium, but I was using them to create fashion and even three-dimensional paintings, if you will. I was playing on texture, colour, and movement, using my floristry skills intertwined with my art skills that I had built up during my life experiences. I would work with materials I had foraged in my yard.

My partner would play his acoustic guitar, and I would create with nature.

I also painted during this time. Painting is always my go-to – painting and music. At this time in my life, I also did a lot of study on floral art and art. I became obsessed with colour theory. I would recite the aspects of it like people recite their times tables when learning them. I really wanted to wrap my head around it, get a clear understanding of how it affected emotion and moods. I was fascinated by how the correct use of colour could make people instantly feel or connect to something. I must have borrowed every book I could from the library on colour theory. I printed charts and colour palettes and stuck them everywhere I could in my tiny house.

I also bought a camera during this lockdown stage of my life. I captured light and started doing my own creative shoots, not really playing with others at this stage as I wasn't well enough. Instead, I was planning out every little fine detail to create a set by myself. I would also shoot the belly ruffles of flowers, the edge of a leaf as the light shone through it, little insects going about the day at the bottom of the garden bed. I loved the little details that might otherwise go unnoticed.

Music was also my healer. Good music can transport me to a beautiful place and make a long journey short. And I did a lot of walking along the beach, long open stretches of fresh salt air, no perfume, no car fumes; just nature. Pure and clean. The beach was my church.

Around the same time, I was fortunate enough to build a strong relationship with Steve White, the CEO of Tesselaar Flowers, one of Australia's largest flower suppliers. He was a magnificent man, and he inspired me in an area where I needed inspiration. He was logical, he was a businessman. We struck a deal: I would create beautiful images for him, and he would share through his avenues. They had to represent his brand, they had to be quality, and they had to be polished to perfection. In return for these elements, he let me be as creative as I wanted to be. He saw the art in me.

Facebook was just new on the scene, and Steve was looking to connect to his clients through

it. He had the product, and I had the talent. I would pitch wild and fantastical ideas to him, and he wasn't worried about knocking me back. I worked closely with his tech guy, Seamus, a fabulous creative tech nerd who was a true artist at heart. (He actually used to be in a famous rock band.) Seamus and I would spend hours on the phone every week coming up with concepts and ways to push the Tesselaar brand in the eyes of the public. The concepts we came up with had to be of value to all: Tesselaar, the viewers, and me. We needed it to be owned by the people who would see it; we wanted to give them a brand or a piece they could connect with and call their own. Whether it just made them smile, inspired them to create, or inspired them to buy flowers, it had to be inspirational for the viewer.

I would create my wearable pieces because I loved them; people connected with that and could see the passion. We also came up with the concept of the "RockStar Florists" competition. People could send in their designs in three categories: Bouquets, Installations, and Wearables. We would post them on Facebook for all to see and be inspired by.

The judges, including me, would choose a winner each day for 10 days; 30 finalists would then go to public vote.

The prize was to spend a day with the RockStar judges, a day of creativity, where we built a suspended installation, created a bouquet, and finished with a wearable fresh flower piece, all captured by photographers. It was a huge hit, and we received more than 2,500 stunning entries. The whole concept was inspirational. It encouraged people to create, and it encouraged discussion. We had more than 1 million hits on social media during this period, which was HUGE back then. It really hit all the nails on the head, giving back to the people with pretty pictures; to florists with education; to Tesselaars with promotional value; and to me, with creative freedom.

Another way I kept myself entertained during my bubble period was by studying. I love creating so much, but I love learning, too. So I studied and worked on getting my qualification in education to become a teacher and a qualified trainer in floristry.

BACK OUT
IN THE WORLD

After nearly two years of being a bubble girl, I started venturing back out into the world, little bit by little bit. My doctors told me that if I locked down and led a very clean and fresh lifestyle – fresh foods only, nothing from a bottle, packet, or can – after 18 months, my immune system would reboot and I would start to tolerate certain chemicals. This was true, to a certain extent.

I had to brave up and start testing myself, to be honest. When I first started out, I was petrified I was going to die on every outing. I suffered a few anxiety attacks, which was reasonable after years of not being able to mix with the general public.

I would drive with my mum in the car, and all of a sudden, the traffic on the highway would come to a solid halt, a thick traffic jam. I would instantly panic and feel my throat closing. I'd cry and have to do breathing exercises to calm myself. But each time it got a little better – I'm happy to report I never once died! – and eventually, I became more confident to venture out into the world.

In addition to all my creating during my bubble years, I also studied and worked on getting my qualification in education to become a teacher and a qualified floristry trainer. Once I was comfortable enough, I started teaching at the college, TAFE. I taught in the science lab because it was a sterile environment. I taught certificate one and two in floristry and introduction to floristry. I would lay my EpiPen out on my desk and show all the students what to do if something bad did happen. Thankfully, it never did. Everyone was so lovely and accommodating.

I taught my students the basics, from colour theory to getting their eyes in line. We'd start with buttonholes, bows and single flowers, then adventure into posy boxes, A-frame designs, and on through to Strauss bouquets. They'd learn the difference between a negative- and positive-spaced design. All of the fundamentals. The most popular class was always the "Nature Session," where I would have the ladies bring a collection of botanical goods – wood, moss, shells, bark, vines, and the like. They would gather interesting greenery. Their pieces would contain minimal flowers, but this was always where their first creative individual was unleashed.

I found that the people who were coming to these sessions were beginners, often young women who were just starting in the flower industry or older women who had always wanted to be florists but had been unable due to the financial aspects of it. Both sets

of these women were like sponges, soaking up the creative process. They loved it!

The funny thing was that I found the older women who had always dreamt of being florists were so creative in a different way. The career paths they had taken were in professional industries that make a lot of money but that are not always as creative or as expressive – especially for someone who has a passion for floristry. These women had focused on their careers, but they all had a need or desire to be a florist – an unbridled passion that was inspirational. I wanted to nurture and enjoy this passion. I wanted to give them opportunities to create like they always wanted to create. So, it was for them that I started booking big gigs – community gigs, gigs that were just for the public, gigs where we got to make fantastical designs – pieces like they'd always dreamt of. We'd do large events – florally abundant – and they evolved from there. I was able to create for the pure sake of creation, but it also led to inspiration in others. This brought me joy.

FLORAL FASHION
ON A GRAND SCALE

I expanded into wearable floristry, but not that of the traditional wearable floristry, which is inspired by fashion. I leaned toward wearable floristry that was inspired by emotion. It was a different game. We made gowns that hit the runways of the international fashion scene, gowns that walked many red-carpet events.

We also did art and large media campaigns as well as lots of high-profile events. We hit the runway of International Fashion Week, opening the show, taking the covers of the local papers, making the news and being featured in many magazines.

I've designed for art festivals, music festivals, and countless fashion shows, from big shiny rooms and red carpets to V.I.P. events, garden festivals and nightclubs.

That can be super exciting and glamorous, but it also takes a lot of dedication and can make

for very long days and nights of building. Making gowns and wearables out of perishable products is always last-minute. They are momentary pieces, which is what makes them so fantastical. I am crazy about details. They MUST look their best under the hot lights of the stage or sitting long hours under set lights, especially given that this is where they will be photographed to be shared with the world. Every beautiful detail will show up in photos; so will every bad detail at a live event where I don't have control over the photographer's viewpoint. So every detail must be perfect.

Which means you prep for weeks on end, then boom! The day of the show is upon you, and it's all stations go. You ship all your products, flowers, frameworks and accessories the night prior to the show. After a long day of preparing for the build, you're in bed by midnight if you are lucky, then up at 3 or 4 a.m. working in the bathroom of a hotel until it's a reasonable time to venture on to the location.

You build a magnificent piece, ready to be enjoyed by all or placed on the model to hit the red carpet or runway. You are now ready to pass out, but no! This is the time you must meet and greet. Adrenaline kicks in, and people's excitement rubs off on you, which is just marvellous. There is no greater joy for me as an artist than to have people enjoy my creations.

Then, just like that, it's all over, and it feels like it's time to pass out. You head back to your room, and it looks like a tree has exploded in it. Greenery, flowers, scissors, wires, and scraps, from one side to the other, your makeup kit strewn over the bathroom sink. The floor is covered in back lining, taped down with heavy tape. It looks like something of a crime scene - a beautiful crime scene.

You choose to ignore it and curl up in bed and fall asleep watching a random midnight movie as a little green spider crawls across your crisp white doona and a praying mantis dances on top of the TV set. You rise like a vampire, eyes burning in the sunlight. You and your team clean the room, gifting any and all leftover flowers to grateful hotel staff, who help you

"A full sensory piece of art, a piece
of you, shared with the world.
This makes it all worth it."

clean up whilst enjoying your tale of the piece. The joy of the creation is fantastic! That achievement of bringing something inside of your head out, sharing it with many to see, touch, and smell. A full sensory piece of art, a piece of you, shared with the world. This makes it all worth it.

You head home and sleep for two days straight, curled up in a nest of pillows and doonas, with

the blinds drawn, only emerging for food and to sit in the shower. Day three arrives, and that sense of joy and excitement fills you, and you start plotting your next design. It is addictive. The vision is inside of you, and you have no choice but to breathe life into it, whether it be for a large, glamorous event viewed on location by many or created at home for the animals to enjoy, shared with the world via the web.

Every event was magnificent and so much fun. I must say I am a sucker for the creative wild ride. I love it. I yearn for it. Sometimes I can't function without it. I will become so caught up in a concept that I will not eat or sleep until it is complete. I can run on two hours of sleep a night for a month, but then I must hibernate.

But the magic we make is truly awe inspiring for me and those who view it.

I once created a large design for an entrance at an arts showcase. The event featured all sorts of media, from the runway to traditional canvas paintings and sculptures.

The building it was held in was an old underground theatre. You walked in through a cave-like entrance. This entrance space was dimly lit, and heavy black paint sat moodily on the walls. Once inside, the venue opened up. It was a large space with spiral staircases and cantilever balconies. It was beautiful. But guess where they put me? Right at the entrance as a feature WOW piece.

So, I decided to work with the space and create a large overgrown Sleeping Beauty installation, complete with a four-poster bed covered in a mass of vines. I featured moody colours to really dramatise the set – red spider orchids that were little art pieces in themselves set against massed dirty-purple-toned Hydrangea. It was magical and moody at the same time. The whole design was based with a mass of deep dark greenery, countless types, to create a delicious texture and give a sense of depth to the piece. I even had a live breathing model lie in the piece. I had my makeup artist paint her ghostly white, with the palest of pink lips and heavy rouge on her cheeks. I built her into the design. She lay there for four hours.

I, as the artist, sat in the corner and listened to people discuss the piece. I was like a creep in the dark, exhausted and intrigued, namelessly enjoying the people viewing my design. They critiqued it without care of offending; they were in awe and discussed all of the elements they loved, opening my eyes to different perspectives. They even tried to figure out if the model was real.

"Stay true to you,
but improve your
skill level."

I loved it. I learned what they enjoyed and what they weren't so keen on.

Personally, I don't think you can improve as an artist unless you listen to critique, take it in, digest it, and take the elements you need to grow from it. Stay true to you, but improve your skill level.

I've always loved these words from Pablo Picasso: "Learn the rules like a pro, so you can break them like an artist."

Once you learn the techniques, injecting your own style of creativity is the next natural step.

ON
THE
FARM

As much as I loved this work, during all of this fancifulness, I lost my touch with the people. It became a whirlwind of high society and high-paced work for many years. When my health began to suffer again, I stepped back. During the peak of it all, I made the decision to step away and move to a farm. Health was key. Without health, I had nothing.

I packed it all up and moved to the hills. All my friends thought I was crazy. They said, "Why are you doing this? You are so successful at the moment. It's crazy!" But I knew it was something that I had to do. I moved to a farm where I eventually collected an abundance of rescue animals. They brought me joy.

I was back in nature. I bought three white chickens. Unable to tell them apart, I used food dye to colour them - blue, green and purple. Weird and strange things like that make me smile.

The next animal to enter the farm was a rooster named Hook. He had been dumped down the road. He walked up our driveway, covered in ticks, very unwell. He was huge. He stood tall, to the top of my thigh. He seemed thankful to be welcomed. I cleaned him up, and he lived with us.

"He watched me with intrigue whilst all of the chickens and guinea fowl gathered around the aviary and watched him..."

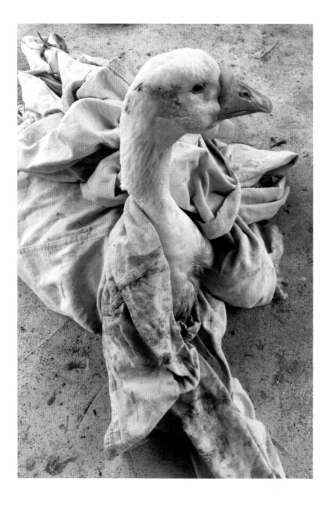

Next came Lewis, a beautiful and very large goose. Lewis came to us through fate. I believe he was destined to live on our little farm. At the crack of dawn one summer day, I woke to my partner tapping on my bedroom window. Half asleep, I rose and sleepily wandered out to him. As he took off for work, he said, "There's something in the aviary for you. Bye!"

Intrigued, I headed straight over to the aviary to find this darling boy, Lewis, covered in blood. He had been dumped down at the end of our street and had obviously had a rough night. He was frightened and injured. I had zero experience with geese, and this boy was huge!

I ran inside, grabbed a bowl of warm water, a few clothes and a little stool.

I approached the poor beautiful creature, who was obviously exhausted and scared. I proceeded to bathe him whilst talking to him in calm, low tones. He became more at ease as if he knew he was now safe. I wrapped a sheet around him to keep him warm, gave him food and water, and let him settle in.

Then I googled "How to look after a goose," reading to him in a play-school-toned voice, trying to sound warm and inviting. He watched me with intrigue whilst all of the chickens and guinea fowl gathered around the aviary and watched him, curious as to who this new creature was on their farm.

A few days later, we let him out to free range on the farm, and he settled in beautifully with all of the other animals.

Lewis now has many little "grand chickens" that he loves dearly and protects – sometimes a little too much. He was best mates with our rescue rooster, Hook, and he roams with the guinea fowl throughout the paddocks. Lewis is patriarch and protector of all our farm babies; a guard goose and, generally, just a beautiful soul. He is very noisy and bossy, but we love him for his outgoing nature.

It always makes me sad to think that someone dumped him. But now, I think he is exactly where he is meant to be. And I also think he is amazingly deserving of the extravagant flower crown he wears in the Lewis print I created. It fills me with joy to say that Lewis now has a "wife," Mildred. She, too, is a rescue baby.

On the farm, I dove into my art and let it wrap around me. I designed large, over-the-top, decadent pieces. Theatrical and fanciful! Pieces that were inspired by nature, music, theatre and the arts – all the things that brought me joy. Again, I created these pieces purely to make my heart happy. I didn't care what others thought. It's said that people can see passion. For years, I thought that was just a common saying. But now, I know it's true. When you create something because you love creation, people see it, people feel that, people connect with it. People were seeing my happiness, my passion, a little part of my soul. I intertwined nature into my

pieces. I worked with all sorts of botanicals. I collected the feathers from my farm babies. I took inspiration from my surrounds.

At this stage, I was heavily focused on wearables. Flowers were my medium. I would lather a mass of greenery as my base, using a variety of shades and textures to really give me an interesting design before I added the flowers.

I love mixing greenery; one type will never suffice. Greenery tells the story of my design. It is dark and shady. I use lighter elements as highlights, floating whimsical strands of greenery to draw the eyes out from the

"Sweet little garden flowers will sing
a song of love if your technique
and composition are on point."

design to the light. Greenery is the heavy base of my painting. From that, all can shine beautifully. The flowers nestle and float amongst the greenery, adding depth and more texture, and, of course, they cement the colour palette and dramatize the beauty in all of my designs.

As a designer using flowers and botanicals as your medium, you need not be concerned about how large or decadent-looking your designs are; you do not have to feature only expensive designer flowers.

Sweet little garden flowers will sing a song of love if your technique and composition are on point. I focus on colour and texture; those two elements alone make my heart sing.

If you create with passion, people will feel it, from a simple vase or a box design through to a grand entrance piece. The 'Roseicapilla' design featured (on the next page), for example, evolved from discarded feathers and fallen branches that would otherwise have been thrown onto the compost heap.

REMEMBERING POSSUM
AND FINDING HAPPINESS

At one point, life decided to throw me a few consecutive challenges, and the final blow was that my dear little rescue galah, Possum, died. I had rescued this sweet bird at the beginning of a challenging personal journey with in-vitro fertilization, and she came into my life and distracted me. She filled me with joy. My journey with IVF failed, but I was okay with that because I had tried. My life was meant for other things.

When Possum passed away, it broke me in two. I could not do anything apart from create art – art for her memory and my healing. The day after she passed, I sat heavy and in tears. I headed out into the yard and I collected guinea-fowl feathers, chicken feathers, sticks, branches, and fallen debris. I wanted to use raw and earthy hues to represent her wild and free nature. She was cheeky, her family visited her daily, she walked around with the chickens, geese, and guinea fowl. At sunset, she would sneak back into our house via the dog door and sleep inside.

I laid a sheet on the floor of my studio, put on some music and created the "Roseicapilla Collection." *Eolophus roseicapilla* is the binomial name for galahs.

I created floral couture, weaving, stitching, and binding, bringing into play all of my technical skills as a florist, and I combined them with pure imagination and passion. I was challenging myself, making certain the composition and design elements were grand enough to represent the impact that Possum had on me and my life.

I let the art pour through my fingers. I was obsessive; I created an entire collection of grand and wonderful pieces. My art had healed me, and, at last, I could sit with my memories, in peace and gratitude for having had Possum in my life.

To showcase, I invited a group of my favourite creative people to the farm, to bring the collection to life: photographer, makeup, hair, model, and fashion. We roamed the paddocks creating. We laughed, we were inspired, we caught the magic – and we shared it with the world.

The "Roseicapilla Collection" graced the covers of magazines and was featured in an art exhibition. People connected with it. They did not know the tale behind the designs; they're interpretive and subjective to the viewers' lived experiences and their perceptions of the work – as is the case for any art piece.

Eventually, the designs I was creating made their way to magazine covers all over the world. They were featured on all kinds of magazines: fashion, arts, women's culture, but never floristry magazines, until more recently.

The pieces landed on large billboards,
the sides of buses, posters and worldwide
campaigns. It was amazing!

My pieces have obviously evolved. My skills
have become refined, my eye has sharpened.
I treat the images I create now like paintings.
I will choose the colour of the skin, the line of
the jaw, set the background and the textures
of the flowers, all to convey an emotion or
a mood or to tell a tale in a single image.
I paint an image from the very beginning.
I know exactly what it is that I want to
express to the viewers, and I bring those
elements to life, one step at a time, through
selection of colour palette, flowers, botanicals, model, photographer, props and
location.

I am finally doing what I was meant to do,
and people respond to my designs. All of
my experiences in life have shaped and
moulded me to this point of creation. It is
here I am happiest – and I have been here
for many years.

VIGNETTES
OF CREATIVITY

As you can probably tell by now, my creative pursuits don't sit still. And they're constantly changing and evolving so that I'm creating in different ways all the time. What follows is a look at some of my various creations and the stories behind them.

To the Streets

Wearables were one element of what I did when I moved to the farm, but I also started to create pieces that were designed to be encountered and experienced in public. They were immersive and interactive pieces, where I would take people and we would create large pieces on the streets in urban environments, to inspire the public. Not only did they inspire the public, but the teams behind the scenes took away so much inspiration, so much knowledge from these builds. It's just a circle of creativity that keeps on giving. How could I survive without doing that? Without inspiring people, entertaining people, making people smile purely out of joy. I'm sharing my happy. That really does bring me joy, too.

The first and most natural evolution was me taking my wearables to the streets. But first, I must digress and mention Rod, my set and props designer and general all-around assistant. He's my genie; anything I ask for, he can bring to life. He is the fabrications team, floral assistant, gatherer of goods and a shoulder to lean on. I test headpieces on him and flick crazy wild designs at him till one sticks. Rod actually is a musician and builder by trade, so he makes the music and is my sense and sensibility when it boils down to it.

One time, I took one of my models in a large full-length gown onto the streets of Brisbane. Rod's role was to construct a rolling stage for me, a stage with industrial wheels and a big rope that enabled me to drag the stage up and down the busy city streets. The stage also had to fit into the hotel lift and my hotel door with ease.

Let me set the scene: Imagine a beautiful, clean white hotel room; now imagine me turning up with boxes and boxes of greenery, rambling vines, and an abundance of flowers. Not a good match, especially when I've already touched on the fact that the aftermath of any of my design sessions looks like a bomb of greenery exploded.

I enter the room, flowers and greenery stay in boxes. I lay a mass of drop sheets, taking one beautiful room and turning it into a studio space. The stage then gets rolled in, set in position to build on. The greenery starts to spill from the boxes, followed by buckets of beautiful blooms. We then construct the gown, I'd say roughly half to three-quarters of the way. We thickly layer the greenery, creating the movement and feel to the gown. All that is left to add is the flowers. They are like the cherry on top! We head to bed.

At 4 a.m., the team arrives. Model, makeup artist, photographer, etc. We giggle and moan about the fact the sun is not up yet. After a quick gripe, we dive in, bringing all of the final elements together. I show everyone my storyboard and paint them a picture with words of the emotions I want the piece to reflect. I give the makeup artist the brief on colour and hair styling; usually I will help with the final touches of the hairstyles as I intertwine my designs into them. The photographer lurks in the background. I let the model know who it is she has to be, what character I want her to take on. She always has to be big and confident, as the pieces are extravagant. If she is not owning it, the whole thing will not speak. I have had experiences of models being too meek for the pieces, and the pieces have overwhelmed them.

My team and I pull and push the stage until we hit a large central bustling area with a tiny garden off to the side. I slide my frame and base works into the garden, then our model is put into the piece. I build around her, merging her with the design, making the piece fit perfectly to her and the location. Whilst I'm continuing the build, my makeup artist fusses with the model's hair, and the photographer fleets around, capturing it all.

People hustle past on the way to work. Many of them stop and thank me for making their morning. They come back on their lunch breaks to see how the build is evolving.

We all interact with the crowd, discussing the elements of the build, telling them of our hotel room - exploded greenery. They, in turn, tell us what the flowers mean to them. They share their stories and enjoy our creative journey. It is incredible, to say the least.

I have since done this countless times at many events and in many urban areas. It's just wonderful to see people's reactions when they wander down a bustling laneway only to come across a beautiful girl adorned in a gown of fresh flowers – and a bunch of creatives who are excited to share the moment with them.

The Teacher in Me

I still teach. I have workshops. I create my floral fashion on large stages at garden and flower shows around the world. I hold workshops for skilled designers where we discuss colour theory and its roles in design, as well as advanced techniques and general floristry skills. We create pieces individually, but together, all learning from each other, with me as the conductor and they are my muses.

I encourage them to create art and to create in a style that they love and that ignites the fire in their bellies. I'm just there to show them the techniques they need to create my designs. However, I don't want them to replicate my designs. I want them to take the skills that I give them and infuse them with their own flavour. We will all have exactly the same ingredients; we will all use the same base structures, the same accessories, the same tools. But each individual design will come out completely different and unique. Some of the designs will be a little wild and woolly, but designers will walk away with the skills to be able to go home and fine-tune their designs.

My goal is to inspire their creative souls, to teach them how to embrace being unique and not worry about following trends. I want to ignite a sense of artistic confidence and give them the professional skills and knowledge to continue on this journey.

The Floral Army

I've conducted large floral builds two stories high where we've used cranes and had 20 women flower lovers and florists, beginners, experts, and garden lovers alike, all working together to create something magical. I have adorned historical arcades in an abundance of floral designs, creating large pieces and transporting them to the location in the darkness of night. Decadent and unusual, done with an army of volunteers creating all day and night. They take so much inspiration from that and then gain so much knowledge. They give to the public, and they get to see people stop and cry and tell them stories of how these beautiful unexpected designs remind them of their grandmother's garden or a holiday once taken.

I've also been the creative director for a large street event where we had 70 women fly in from around the world to join our floral army and create for a week. Like clockwork, we would gather in the mornings around sketches of the designs that I had drawn up during our briefing. These were on large sheets of butcher paper, hung like scriptures in the dining area. We would stop at midday for lunch and to assess how we were doing. A well-fed team works magically. Food and music make for a happy floral army.

The floral army helped build an abundance of classical floral designs, from garlands to run along the street to large suspended vine balls and everything in between. Even before the floral army had arrived, one very clever artist sculpted a mould of Lewis the goose and a collection of chickens, roosters, and sheep in clay. We cast little farm animals and faces in resin and painted them by hand.

Inside the house, the floors were covered in drop sheets, and we had a team working on headpieces, wearable pieces, garlands, suspended installations, flowers in vials – all of those tiny pieces of the jigsaw puzzle that needed to be individually made and assembled on location.

VIGNETTES OF CREATIVITY   **77**

Each team knew what they were doing, numbering each element of their design. And like the conductor of some great theatre performance, I knew exactly what each team was doing and what they were up to.

We installed our pieces under the cover of night and had the street wake up to our floral magnificence. It was something I'll never forget.

10,000 Flowers

One immersive design I created consisted of more than 10,000 paper flowers. The flowers were made from obsolete books from the public library, which were about to be thrown into recycling. We took those books and asked the public to help us create 10,000 paper flowers, in black-and-white only, as I wanted to introduce colour with lighting. I created templates that were easily achievable for people of all dexterity levels. People created the flowers over a three-month period.

During this time, Rod, my best mate who does all the fabrications, built a false room approximately 10 metres long by about 3-and-a-half metres wide, which he painted black and installed on location. We then completely enclosed the room with curtains. I spent a month with my volunteers filling the room with the 10,000 flowers. Rod then came back and installed coloured lights, a sound system and an essential-oil infuser. I wanted to take away people's senses by making the room dark, then excite their senses again by introducing each

"My goal is to inspire their creative souls, to teach them how to embrace being unique and not worry about following trends."

element. I set the temperature in the room low, as it was hot summer day outside. I infused essential oils of vanilla, for old books, and eucalyptus, because it was in Australia. I introduced lighting in single colours into sections of the designs. People walked in and through the piece and back out the other side, with all their senses engaged.

25,000 Butterflies

During COVID, I wanted to create something that would inspire people, something that people could still be part of whilst in isolation.

The first part of this particular piece was to get people to create simple paper butterflies at home and send them to us, giving us a way to be connected. The goal was for 10,000 butterflies. I thought this might be a lofty goal but wanted to aim for the stars. People had three weeks to get them to me. We received 25,000 butterflies, all with letters of how the butterflies inspired the makers. Amazing! I know that touched a lot of hearts, including mine.

The second element of the design was a shipping container. It was dropped to my farm, and we painted the outside with interactive paintings, pieces that people would stand by and have their photos taken. The 25,000 butterflies lived inside the container. We built a grotto from papier-mâché and a beautiful floral set. I introduced lighting into the space for mood. The piece was supposed to have theatre curtains on the outside through which people were supposed to enter, but, unfortunately, due to COVID, the curtains had to be removed. Even so, people were able to walk inside and experience the piece. For the times, it was incredibly moving.

Flowered Faces

Alongside the large builds I create, I also do quirky and fun builds. For example, there is a large city-meets-country show at which I conduct a flower-beard build on stage. We have a famous Aussie with a beard. He comes along and gets his beard flowered. Then we pair a bunch of everyday blokes with florists. The florists get one hour to flower beards. I hold a workshop the night before to show the florists some tricks, as they're putting flower beards on strangers who have to wear them for hours on end in a public spotlight. Although it may be a laugh, they need to make their models comfortable and their designs durable.

The day of the beard build, the public votes and the designers and everyday blokes get to walk in the grand parade, with 10,000 animals, whilst everyone cheers. This event brings so many smiles to so many people. It's a hoot and giggle, but these ladies have real skills.

MAKING
THE
MAGIC

With anything I create, there is my own inspiration and interpretation. No two pieces are the same, and neither is the process on any of my creations. That said, there are certain elements of design that typically go into every one of my works. Elements of design are the building blocks; they provide the structure for a design or an artwork.

POP

Colour - When I conceptualised this piece, I wanted a bright colour palette. It had to pop and be fun.

Shape and Form - Strangely enough, I introduced a non-botanical element here. I needed it to be rigid and bright to emphasise a solid repetitive form. It had to be circles – circles running from the ear to the shoulders, drawing a line. Circular but linear at the same time. I repeated the grouped solid circular forms in the hair to give a sense of balance to the design. However, I intentionally exposed the edges of the circles, which softens them. This took a solid piece and made it a negative space.

Line - The structure of the collar emphasises the line. The florals featured on the top line of the shoulder are intentionally soft, so as not to distract from the shape and form of the earrings. By keeping the medium used in the shoulder line soft, the two elements are connected, as opposed to making them compete for one's attention. Also, the "V" of the design is heavy, giving a sense of balance and settling the eyes.

Space - An intentional negative space has been left, exposing the model's collar bone. This negative space is a key element to the design, as it gives the piece its form.

Texture - The contrasting textures of the soft massed florals set against the hard definitive look of the jewellery are what sets the two apart when it comes to line. They draw the eyes through the piece with comfort and ease.

Floral Artist - @flowersbyjuliarose
Photographer - @paulharris
Makeup and Hair - @alishahennessymakeup
Model - @hannahtompkins_
Jewellery - @flockcuriosityassembly
Location - 11Past11Studio; Currumbin, Gold Coast, Queensland

THE WILDFLOWER

In the heart of Tokyo, I created this with a collection of designer flowers intertwined with gorgeous little wildflowers gathered from a private garden in Chiba Prefecture.

We designed this piece for a World Flower Council demonstration in Japan. After the design had adorned the stage, we packed the piece into a big, old, well-used suitcase that was sturdy and had a good set of wheels. We lugged the suitcase up and down – and up and down – the stairs on the Tokyo underground rail loop until we reached our set location. The city was alive, bustling, and filled with constant energy.

A small team of creatives stood waiting for us at a busy intersection: the photographer, from Europe; the model and makeup artist, both from Japan; and me, the floral couture designer from Australia. We had never met before, and none of us spoke fluently in each other's language. We did, however, speak the language of art.

We wandered down to a small nature strip set on a side street. There, we opened the suitcase, and the model stepped into the flowered gown. Then we took a few moments to capture the magic of a wildflower in the heart of Tokyo.

Floral Artist - @flowersbyjuliarose
Photographer - @elenatyutina
Makeup and Hair - @makeuphitomi
Model - @mari_hirao

COMMANDETTE

When conceptualising this piece, I envisioned an abundance of lush greenery.
I wanted the main element to be a delightful, delicious, and decadent mixture
of textures.

The greenery was layered from dark to light, dramatising the depth of the
design and colour palette. The lower section of the design was wild but simple,
emphasising green en masse.

At the top of the piece, I introduced a mixture of berries, tight little flower pods,
and nuts. These elements really accentuate the texture in the piece. The minimal
amount of feature roses is purely to intensify the rich colour palette and settle
the eyes of the viewers. Rich in colour, abundant yet subtle, wild but contained.

Floral Artist - @flowersbyjuliarose
Photographer - @ingridcolesphoto
Makeup and Hair - @alishahennessymakeup
Model - @savannahfineform
Painting - @llewellyn_skye_art
Greenery Supplier - @djirangplantation

THE HOLLOW

I challenged myself when creating this piece. I wanted to design a magnificent shape. I needed this piece to be more than an opulent orchid headpiece. It had to twist and curve, drawing the eyes from the headpiece to the shoulder piece in a connected but not overwhelming way. The form had to be correct to create the emotion I wanted in the design.

The headpiece itself is heavier in flowers, with individual wired *Cymbidium* orchids grouped on this section of the design. The orchids then scatter as they trail to the back of the design. Fresh-picked moss features between the blooms. The moss emphasises the sense of space. This element leads viewers' eyes through the design into the negative space between the body and the design. This leading line gives the design its depth.

The piece then wraps back around the model, becoming heavier in *Cymbidium* orchids, continuing the lush, thickened base of moss.

This form was very hard to achieve. It was the challenge that excited me as an artist and a designer. Throw in the comfort for the model, and the challenge gets harder. But I love it. It's like a Rubik's Cube of flowers.

From conception to life. It starts as an idea - "I wonder... ?" - then pours through my hands for hours and hours on end until that idea, that vision, is real, standing in front of me, to share with everyone.

Floral Artist - @flowersbyjuliarose
Photography - @bonniecee
Makeup and Hair - @ans_thats_it_
Model - @karlabodycote

FLORAL SWING

I designed this with a mixture of native Australian flowers. These gorgeous flowers were set in an abundance of fresh foraged greenery from my farm.

I created this piece for the Botanical Bazaar Gardening Expo. It hung proudly from a branch in a big old tree for all to enjoy. The scent of eucalyptus swirled around the people as they sat inside the piece, surrounded by beautiful blooms. It was lovely.

Flowers speak a language that can be enjoyed by all.

Floral Artist – @flowersbyjuliarose
Photography – @cloudcatcherstudio
Makeup – @sugarmobilemakeup
Model – @jasminpenwarn

VEE VEE

Shapes can be used in art to control one's feelings about the mood and composition of an artwork. In this piece, note that the triangular shape on the shoulder is the same size as the missing "V" in the design. Even though the design is heavily offset, it still has a sense of balance.

The texture is suppressed to allow the expressive qualities of shape and colour to flourish. An analogous colour palette was used to emphasise the calmness of emotion. However, hues in the colour palette were shifted to add a pop.

The balance gives the viewer a sense of calmness whilst the angles create an edge to the design. The colour, bright with soft overtones, completes the feel.

———————————————————

Floral Artist - @flowersbyjuliarose
Photography - @cloudcatcherstudio
Makeup and Hair - @alishahennessymakeup
Model - @classandcolor__

KOREL

This design is tinkering on the edge of monochromatic and analogous in the colour field. Even though the colours of the flowers are so close, it's the unique and interesting blend of textures that makes each individual colour really pop.

To take it one step further, the soft and velvety blooms set against the hard, strong line of the spear grass injects extra emphasis on the texture.

Created at the Melbourne International Flower and Garden Show.

Floral Artist - @flowersbyjuliarose
Photography - Jose Gonzalez @hossay
Makeup - @alishahennessymakeup
Model - @maki.m0use

ROCK IT

A little rock and a little glam – all whilst being fabulously decadent and designer.
We shot this in a laneway at night. It's gritty and dark – all barbed-wire
fencing and broken asphalt. The smoke bomb sets the rock atmosphere whilst
the dewy makeup says "I'm glam." A designer gown seems out of place, but
it works perfectly set amongst an abundance of *Phalaenopsis* orchids, roses,
and rambling vines.

I created this during a workshop for Tesselaar's "RockStar Florists" competition.

_____

Floral Artist - @flowersbyjuliarose
Photography - @cloudcatcherstudio
Makeup - @bexi_makeupartist
Hair - @amyspryhair
Gown - @begitta
Model - @_zoeleung

BLUSH

Soft, feminine, and a little Victorian, this piece was set on the farm. To capture the right lighting, we headed out into one of the paddocks, wandering around until we found the perfect setting.

Soft green branches, dappled light, and the babbling brook set the mood. It was time to shoot: floral couture in position, camera loaded, model perfect. We were ready to make a little magic.

Halfway through our magic making, a momma cow, who had just had a calf (and was a little protective), decided she was not picking up the magic vibe as much as we were. She wanted us out of the paddock. With momma cow hot on our heels, we quickly grabbed all our goods and hightailed it across the paddock. We rolled under the farmyard fence with urgency, and momma cow eased up, turned around, and went back to her bubba.

Needless to say, the rest of the shoot was carried out inside the fenced area, under a big old jacaranda tree.

A little bit of adventure is always good for the soul – and getting chased by a cow always puts a spark in your step.

_____

Floral Artist - @flowersbyjuliarose
Photography - @caseyjane_photography
Makeup - @kyliesprofessional
Model - @s0phiamay

REFEL

This piece of floral couture was created for the people. I envisioned it as interactive art, made to mingle and be photographed with the crowds.

We'd finished our work and had no need to stay on at the show. But honestly, why would we want to leave a flower and garden festival in full swing? We were exhausted but wanted to stay and play. I whipped up this piece, and our whole team roamed, laughed, and talked with the public.

Being able to talk with strangers and hear people tell you their tales of gardens, flowers, and where their joy of nature springs from. I love doing this; it brings me joy. I can't wait to do it again.

Captured in a sun shower at the Melbourne International Flower and Garden Show, 2019.

Floral Artist - @flowersbyjuliarose
Photography - @fiafiaart_branding
Makeup - @alishahennessymakeup
Model - @bellabirdiie
Location - Carlton Gardens, Melbourne

MATZAH

The story behind the piece? I was inspired to create it as I drove my tiny hire car around the streets of the tropics.

It seemed that everywhere I looked, my eyes were caught by an abundance of yellow hanging flowers, swaying in the hot, balmy breeze. Then the tropical rains would hit, and the flowers would fall to the ground, leaving golden puddles.

I wanted to share this beauty.

At the time, I was in North Queensland for some of my floral workshops. During one session, we had created a fully wired flower crown. I used this as a starting point. The rest of the base was designed late at night whilst watching a movie and eating Indian takeout in my hotel suite.

I completed the bulk of this piece on location, where I stood by the back door of my little hire car with nothing but a few wires, some Parafilm, and pair of floral scissors. The little flowers I used, once picked, last but just a moment. They're fragile, so they're not good cut flowers.

This image has won photographic awards in the U.S., graced magazine covers internationally, and has been featured in countless editorials - yet it comes from such humble beginnings. Even though the piece itself is quite decadent, there is nothing decadent or fancy about its creation. It's pure and simple. The piece was born from the love of nature and art combined.

Floral Artist - @flowersbyjuliarose
Photography - @carlykphotography
Makeup - @makeupbycarlyb
Model - @_kana22_
Location - Carlton Gardens, Melbourne
Floral Accessories - @cairnsfloralsupplies

BALUHNS

Technique is always the underlying key to making beautiful things look simple. This crown of *Anthurium* stood tall and slender. The greenery swayed in the gentle breeze, adding a little extra movement to the piece.

The design was large but so beautifully balanced weight-wise that it sat with ease on our model as she walked around the paddocks.

———————————————

Floral Artist - @flowersbyjuliarose
Photography - @photographerkat_fantasy
Makeup - Chelsi Hair and Makeup
Model - Indy Flavelle

INDEX

Page 4 (opposite "Contents" page)
Photo: @hossay
Makeup: @styled_by_nathalie_anne
Model @iam_bazelika_

Drag Queen on Page 5 ("Contents" page)
Photo: @photographerkat
Queen: @thescarlettfever

Girl Leaning on Tree on Page 5 ("Contents" page)
Photo: @intricate_exposures
Model: @itsnatrios

Page 7
Photo: @hossay
Makeup and Hair: @styled_by_nathalie_anne
Model: @claudine_henningsen

Page 8
Photo: @hossay
Makeup and Hair: @styled_by_nathalie_anne
Model: @kristenfebey

Page 11
Photo: @elenatyutina
Makeup and Hair: @makeuphitomi
Model: @mari_hirao

Pages 12, 13
Photo: @intricate_exposures
Model: @itsnatrios

Page 14
Photo: @intricate_exposures
Model: @itsnatrios

Page 16, 17
Photo: @cloudcatcherstudio
Makeup and Hair: @erinstuartstyles
Model: @jessicacavallaro

Pages 18, 19
Photo: @cloudcatcherstudio
Model: @jessicacavallaro

Page 20
Photo: @carlykphotography
Makeup and Hair: @lizaformilan
Model: @_kana22_

Page 21, 22
Photo: @caseyjane_photography
Pink Queen: @itsmisspoodle
Green Queen: @shushufuntanna
Red Queen: @thescarlettfever

Pages 29, 30, 31
Photo: @cloudcatcherstudio
Makeup: @bexi_makeupartist
Hair: @amyspryhair
Model: @_zoeleung

Pages 32, 33, 34, 35
Photo: @carly_tia

Page 36
Photo: @angiebranchphotography

Page 37
Photo: @angiebranchphotography
Makeup and Hair: @vanessasuzette_makeup
Model: @gabbylennon

Pages 38, 39
Photo: @carlykphotography
Makeup and Hair: @lizaformilan
Model: @k.maaay

Pages 40, 41
Photo: @_colin.mclellan_
Model: @mccareytanaya_

Pages 42, 43
Photo: @fiafiaart_branding
Makeup: @styled_by_nathalie_anne
Models: @prisciliagoh, @iam_bazelika_
Clothing: @pazadz

Pages 44, 45
Photo: @carlykphotography
Makeup: @alicemakeupartist
Model: @sodiumisomer

Pages 46, 47
Photo: @carlykphotography
Makeup: @makeupbycarlyb
Hair: @shannoninnergoddess
Model: @_kana22_

Pages 48, 49
Photo: @marquebrandstudio_weddings
Model: @xanthewm
Makeup: @gabriellehoughtonmua
This piece was brought to life in one of Julia Rose's
two-day workshops in New Zealand by attendees
under the creative direction of Julia Rose.
Sponsored by: @nzpflorist

Pages 50, 51
Photo: @paulharris
Makeup and Hair: @alishahennessymakeup
Model: @s0phiamay

Pages 52, 53, 54, 55
Photo: @paulharris
Makeup and Hair: @alishahennessymakeup
Model: @hannahtompkins_

Page 56, 57, 59, 60, 61
Photo: @cloudcatcherstudio

Pages 62, 63
Photo: @nicolalemmonphotos
Makeup and Hair: @alishahennessymakeup
Model: @classandcolor__

Page 64
Photo: @cloudcatcherstudio
Makeup and Hair: @alishahennessymakeup
Model: @classandcolor__

Page 65
Photo: @photographerkat
Red Queen: @thescarlettfever
Pink Queen: @shushufuntanna

Pages 66, 67
Photo: @intricate_exposures
Model: @itsnatrios

Pages 69, 70, 71
Photo: @cloudcatcherstudio
Makeup and Hair: @emilykhair
Model: @missmolliegilbert02

Pages 73, 74
Photo: @ingridcolesphoto
Makeup and Hair: @alishahennessymakeup
Model: @savannahfineform
Painting: @llewellyn_skye_art

Page 74 - bottom
Photo: @angiebranchphotography
Makeup and Hair: @vanessasuzette_makeup
Model: @gabbylennon

Pages 76, 77
Photo: @fiafiaart_branding
Makeup: @styled_by_nathalie_anne
Models: @prisciliagoh @iam_bazelika_
Clothing: @pazadz

Page 78
Photo: @rcstills
Makeup: @alishahennessymakeup
Model: @awhina_anima

Page 79, 80
Photo: @cloudcatcherstudio
Makeup and Hair: @erinstuartstyles
Model: @jessicacavallaro

Page 81
Photo: @ingridcolesphoto

Page 83
Photo: @paulharris
Makeup and Hair: @alishahennessymakeup
Model: @s0phiamay

ACKNOWLEDGMENTS

Thank you to Rod, for the music and for always being my rock and best mate. You are sense and sensibility, grounding me in life. Thank you for the fabrications, the sets, bones and bases. From the small through to the extravagent and grand. I am beyond grateful that you always just have faith in my art and create for me no matter how wild and obscure my concepts or how abstract my sketches may be.

To Ken and Chrissy, for encouraging me to always be myself and never saying no to the late nights and early mornings.

Thanks Steve White, for believing in my art and never trying to change my style.

To Seamus, Clarissa, and Rose, for the hours of creative discussions.

To Sean and Luke, for throwing a hand up whenever I needed you there.

Thanks, Sylvia, for all the words and guidance.

And to the floral armies, for rising up with me and creating beautiful art that inspires and speaks to so many.

Thank you, also, to everyone who saw the unique beauty and passion in my art, including Lynn, June and Rita.

To Jon, for taking my words and fine-tuning them into this tale;
to Kathleen, for bringing this story to life, visually;
and to Travis, for having faith.

Lastly, I'd like to thank you, the reader, for picking up this book and supporting the arts. The world needs more people like you.

Floral Artist - @flowersbyjuliarose
Photographer - @lightpicture_studio
Makeup - @alishahennessymakeup
Model - @katherine__ellen